Ann Coburn
ALEX AND THE WARRIOR
A CHRISTMAS PLAY IN TWO ACTS

OBERON BOOKS
LONDON

First published in 2004 by Oberon Books Ltd
(incorporating Absolute Classics)
521 Caledonian Road, London N7 9RH
Tel: 020 7607 3637 / Fax: 020 7607 3629
e-mail: oberon.books@btinternet.com
www.oberonbooks.com

A catalogue record for this book is available from the British
Library.

ISBN: 1 84002 502 6

Printed in Great Britain by Antony Rowe Ltd, Chippenham.

Cover illustration: Laurence Hutchins '

To obtain the original music written for *Alex and the Warrior* (used
throughout the play), contact NTC Touring Theatre Company
at Alnwick Playhouse, Bondgate Without, Alnwick,
Northumberland, NE66 1PQ.

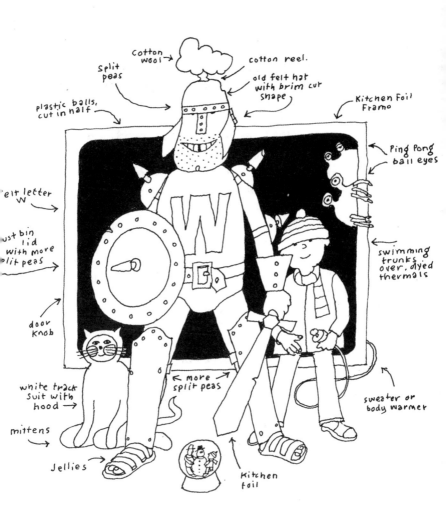

*Illustration and suggestions for staging
by Laurence Hutchins*

Acknowledgements

Thanks to:

Director Gillian Hambleton for taking the play from page to stage with such warmth, intelligence, humour and flair – and a special thank you, Gill, for releasing the snowman from the globe;

Kim Evans, Jackie Fielding, Gary Kitching, Alan Park and Stephen Wedd – a fine group of actors who were so generous with their ideas and enthusiasm during rehearsals and whose superb performances brought *Alex and the Warrior* to life for a whole range of audiences;

Cath Young for being there, in every sense of the phrase, once again;

Robyn Flemming for coming up with some fantastic set and costume ideas and then working so hard to produce them;

Ben Steppenbeck for his calm and efficient stage management and some great lighting effects;

Andy Ross and Trish Havery for set build and wardrobe;

Jim Kitson for some truly excellent original music;

Anna Flood, Hilary Burns and Susan Young, NTC Theatre Group's administration team, for all their hard work behind the scenes.

AC

Characters

ALEX

CAT

SKARG 1

SKARG 2

THE WARRIOR

UBIQUITOUS GRAVEL-VOICED
AMERICAN (UGVA)
in voice-over only

Alex and the Warrior was first performed at Alnwick Playhouse by NTC Touring Theatre Company on 3 December 2003 with the following cast.

ALEX, Alan Park

THE WARRIOR, Gary Kitchins

CAT, Kim Evans

SKARG 1, Stephen Wedd

SKARG 2, Jackie Fielding

Directed by Gillian Hambleton

Designed by Robyn Flemming (Mentored by Cath Young)

Stage Manager, Ben Steppenbeck

Original Music, Jim Kitson

Set Build, Andy Ross

Wardrobe Assistant, Trish Havery

ACT ONE

Scene 1

The five actors enter as a group of carol singers, singing 'Deck the Halls with Boughs of Holly' or similar. They are all wearing hats and scarves. They position themselves around the space and finish the verse. As they stop singing, the first, halting notes of the 'Snow' music begin to play. The five raise their heads and look up as the 'Snow' tune develops (a joyful, crystalline instrumental piece). Snow begins to fall (this can be suggested by, for instance, a turning mirror-ball) and the five all raise their faces and lift their arms to the sky. They hoist a circle of white parachute silk into the air. One of the actors steps under the silk. When the silk falls, the other actors add a hat and scarf to the figure under the silk, turning it into a snowman. A snowball fight ensues, then, as the music fades, the snowman melts away and three of the actors leave the space.

The two remaining actors remove their hats and scarves and become ALEX and CAT. Now the parachute silk has been cleared away, the space becomes ALEX's bedroom. At the back of the acting space there is a large, silver frame. This frame will become various screens and doorways throughout the play. At present it is ALEX's gaming screen. There is also an unimpressive, artificial Christmas tree in a corner and some sort of a stool with a gaming handset beside it. CAT settles on the stool and ALEX picks up a snowstorm containing a man, a boy and a snowman. He shakes it and then watches the snow swirl in the little glass dome. CAT comforts him by rubbing her head against his arm. ALEX strokes CAT for a moment, then stores the snowstorm away. Unceremoniously, he pushes CAT off the beanbag and retrieves his handset. CAT lifts her tail and stalks offstage, highly offended. ALEX collapses onto the beanbag, points the handset at the screen and clicks PLAY. *His mother calls.*

ALEX: Coming, Mum!

ALEX drops the handset and exits, leaving the game still loading.

Scene 2

UGVA, SKARG 1, SKARG 2, WARRIOR

The Skarg music begins to play as the UBIQUITOUS GRAVEL-VOICED AMERICAN (UGVA) sets the scene in voice-over.

UGVA: A land – in peril. A people – in hiding. From the far reaches of space an evil beyond imagining has invaded their world.

Two SKARG enter, hooded and cloaked. Black netting at the front of the hoods makes them seem faceless. There is a suggestion of a pair of bulbous, insect-like eyes on the top of the hoods. Their limbs are long and angular and they move like spiders. Their heads twitch and jerk from side to side as they make their malevolent way across the space.

The Skarg. Shapeshifting killers, their deadliest weapon is disguise. When evil can take any form, there is no safety. There is no escape. Only one man can save his people. Only one man can lead them. He is –

The music swells into a Hollywood hero-theme as the WARRIOR enters and poses heroically. He is dressed something like a Gladiator and he carries a shield and a sword at his belt.

The Warrior!
The Warrior. Never was a hero more needed.
The Warrior. Available in all good stores now.
The Warrior. Are you tough enough?

The SKARG and the WARRIOR go through a choreographed fight sequence and then step through into the large frame at the back of the stage. Once in position, they freeze. Music ends.

Scene 3

CAT
(WARRIOR, SKARG 1, SKARG 2: IN FREEZE-FRAME)

CAT enters and moves in a cat-like way through the audience into the space. She is beautiful, elegant, with pure white fur. An 'every-cat', she can talk in asides to the audience but is not understood by those on stage (although she understands them). She gives the audience the once-over. She is unimpressed.

CAT: I don't need anything today
You can leave now. Go away.
(*An increasingly irritated pause.*)
I see you don't know who I am,
Otherwise you would all scram.
My name is 'Queen Almighty
Sleekest Fur Alrighty
Sharpest Claws In Sighty
Prowling Gardens Nightly
Eyes a-shining brightly
Empress Aphrodite'.
I am a very noble cat.
When I say 'go' you do just that!

CAT sits down and begins to groom herself thoroughly. This can be the traditional groom with the tongue, or it could be a case of getting a comb and mirror out. She is about to get to an intimate bit when she glances up and is annoyed to find the audience still there.

It's Christmas Eve! Now surely you
Can find some other things to do?
Presents don't walk off the shelves
And turkeys never stuff themselves.

She turns her back to carry on grooming and then turns to glare at the audience. She stalks towards them.

I thought I made it very clear
No more servants needed here.
My humans serve me very well.
Besides, you're ugly – and you smell.

A pause, then CAT lifts her tail and shows her rear end. This cat-like gesture of disdain can be as literal or interpretative as desired. Suddenly CAT turns back to the audience.

Unless you've come to worship me…?
Of course! You've heard my poetry!
All cats can rhyme, but I'm the best.
I leave the doggerel to the rest.
'The cat sat on the mat' – that's mine.
An early effort. Unrefined.
Catchy, yes, but far too short.
Not like my later, epic sort.
They go on all night for hours!
I'll sing you one, but, please, throw flowers.
Not shoes, alarm clocks or false teeth.
I know you mean well but, good grief,
Those things can really hurt, you know!
You ought to think before you throw.
Your species really is quite dense.
Not an ounce of common sense!
Take Alex. When I talk to him
He acts as though he's listening.
He pricks his ears and tilts his head
He really doesn't look brain-dead.
But he can't even learn my name.
Too long for him. It's such a shame.
Instead, he calls me Sn…Sn… Oh!
I can't repeat it. On we go.
My poem. 'To a hunter's moon.'
Sing along, if you know the tune.

CAT begins to yowl wordlessly in a dreadful, off-key way. Her performance is interrupted in mid-caterwaul by…

Scene 4

CAT, ALEX
(WARRIOR, SKARG 1, SKARG 2: IN FREEZE-FRAME)

…ALEX's explosive entrance.

ALEX: (*Shouting to his mother, off-stage.*) I'm not going!

CAT: (*Aside to audience.*) Alex. My human. He's upset.
His Grandad had to see the vet.
'Doctor', I think you humans say.
The vet told him he had to stay
In something called a 'hospital'
Until he's back to feeling well.

ALEX: Stupid hospitals! I hate them! (*Shouting to off-stage.*)
And I'm not visiting Grandad in there!

ALEX listens but there is no answer.

Did you hear me? Mum…?

Still no answer.

She's gone. Mum's gone to the hospital without me.

ALEX picks up the snowstorm containing a man and a boy building a snowman. He shakes it and watches the snow swirl. He talks both to himself and to CAT but without expecting any reply or understanding from her.

It's Christmas Eve! Grandad always takes me into town on Christmas Eve. The shops are open late and there's loads of stuff going on in the main square. Someone from the telly always does the countdown for the start of the fancy dress parade. And this year there's a skating pond in the park. Grandad would've liked the pond.

CAT watches ALEX. Her obvious affection and increasingly frequent glances of concern contradict her words.

CAT: Humans! More trouble than they're worth.
  Who'd have 'em? Drown them all at birth!
  My wise old mother used to say,
  'A scratch a day keeps the human away.'

ALEX: Why can't Christmas be like it used to be? Dad
  knew how to do Christmas. He always bought a real tree
  and put loads of decorations on it.

*ALEX gives the little artificial tree a disgusted look, then
shakes the snowstorm again*

And when it snowed, me and Dad always used to build
the best snowman in the street. We built a whole family
once – even a cat! They were brilliant – all with different
faces. Christmas was great when Dad was here. It's going
to be rubbish, this year.

*ALEX slumps on the stool. CAT looks at ALEX, keeps moving
a little closer.*

CAT: Strict and haughty, that's the style.
  Give them an inch and they'll take a mile.
  Trouble is, he's really sweet.
  So little fur. Such clumsy feet.
  And he's so clever with his hands.

Finally giving in and rubbing against him.

Sometimes I think he understands
Every single word I say –

ALEX: Oh, Snowball…

*CAT pulls away from ALEX and sits bolt upright, turning a
scandalised face to the audience.*

CAT: – but that'll be the day.

*CAT chokes as ALEX grabs her, gripping her tightly around
the neck as he drags her around the space after him. She spits*

and splutters, struggling to get away from his stranglehold, but ALEX is too upset to notice.

ALEX: Grandad can't be in hospital on Christmas Eve! It's all wrong. We have to do something, Snowball!

CAT manages to break away. Glowering and hissing, she gives ALEX a glare, then lifts her tail and shows her rear end.

Oh, charming. Thanks for all your help. Stupid cat.

CAT stalks to the other side of the space. ALEX turns his back on her, picks up his games handset and points it at the screen.

Scene 5

WARRIOR, SKARG 1, SKARG 2, CAT, ALEX, UGVA

UGVA: A land – in peril. A people – in hiding. Only one man can save them. The Warrior. Are you tough enough?

On-screen, the 'hero' music plays as WARRIOR and the SKARG come to life. Staying within the screen, WARRIOR and the SKARG move into action complete with arcade-game style sound effects. Their faces expressionless, they stage a stylised fight with slow, jerky movements which is, frankly, pathetic after the earlier big build up. One SKARG goes down, but WARRIOR is badly wounded. When the second SKARG attacks, WARRIOR staggers, then falls. ALEX throws down his handset and stands up, turning his back on the screen.

Game over, Warrior. You scored a measly nine hundred points, buying only ninety of your people their freedom.

ALEX: Only ninety! That sounds pretty good to me. I can't even rescue one. If I really was a hero like the Warrior,

I'd be tough enough to do anything. I'd fight my way into that hospital and bust Grandad out of there!

ALEX makes a few martial arts fighting moves, complete with accompanying noises, before coming to a stop.

That would be brilliant!

Realising the unreality of his fantasy, ALEX slumps and picks up the snowstorm.

UGVA: New game. Are you ready to try again?

Behind ALEX the WARRIOR rises to his feet again and stands ready.

ALEX: (*Shaking the snowstorm.*) I wish it were that easy. I wish the Warrior could be real.

Something starts to happen behind ALEX. Music begins to play. The Christmas tree rises up into something much more impressive and arcs of power come from the screen, but ALEX does not notice. He is staring intently into the snowstorm.

I wish he could step out of the game.
I wish he could come and bust Grandad out of hospital for me.

With each wish ALEX makes, the magic grows. The WARRIOR seems to hear something. He steps up to the screen and peers out. The Christmas tree is transformed into something magical. The lights flare up ten times more brightly, the decorations shiver and clink.

CAT: Alex. Turn around and see –

ALEX: Stop yowling, Snowball.

CAT: Something's happening to the tree!

ALEX: I said shut up, you stupid cat! You've been fed!

CAT yowls and backs away as smoke fills the screen (the SKARG should take this opportunity to get out of sight for now). ALEX finally realises something is happening as the lights and noise reach a crescendo. He turns as the WARRIOR steps out through the screen. ALEX is totally astounded but the WARRIOR is calm and alert, drawing his sword and checking his surroundings for danger. CAT is hiding behind ALEX as WARRIOR quarters the space, looking for SKARG. He spots CAT.

WARRIOR: I see it!

CAT again tries to hide behind ALEX.

Get down boy!

ALEX ducks just in time to avoid being decapitated by the swinging sword as the WARRIOR lunges for CAT, sword aloft.

ALEX: No! That's Snowball!

ALEX manages to throw himself in front of CAT just before WARRIOR brings the sword crashing down onto her.

WARRIOR: It is a Skarg! They take many forms.

Again, WARRIOR brings the sword down and CAT just manages to leap clear.

ALEX: (*Pursuing WARRIOR.*) No! It's a cat! She's a cat!

ALEX jumps in front of CAT for a second time. WARRIOR pauses, his sword still raised.

WARRIOR: Not a Skarg?

ALEX: No!

A disappointed WARRIOR lowers his sword. Cautiously CAT recovers her dignity and lifts her tail at the WARRIOR before stalking off.

ALEX: She's just an animal.

WARRIOR: (*Brightening.*) Meat!

>*WARRIOR raises his sword and again prepares to kill CAT.*

ALEX: No! She's a pet!

WARRIOR: Apet? What is Apet?

ALEX: She – belongs to me.

CAT: I don't belong to you, you knave!
   I'm the owner. You're the slave.

WARRIOR: What is the purpose of this belonging of yours?

>*CAT reacts with frustration that they cannot understand her.*

ALEX: Well –

WARRIOR: (*With actions.*) Does this belonging guard your
   dwelling?

ALEX: Well, no.

WARRIOR: (*With actions.*) Does it hunt for you?

ALEX: Not as such, no…

WARRIOR: (*With actions.*) Does it fight for you?

ALEX: She fights other cats sometimes – but not for me.

>*The WARRIOR shrugs and raises his sword again. CAT yowls.*
>*ALEX stops the WARRIOR for the third time.*

ALEX: No, you mustn't kill her!

WARRIOR: But this belonging has no use – except as meat.

ALEX: She's my pet! I love her!

WARRIOR: What is love? Does it have a use?

ALEX: Yes, it has a use. It's… It's… Oh, it doesn't matter! Snowball is not a Skarg. There are no Skarg here.

WARRIOR: No Skarg?

ALEX: None at all.

WARRIOR: Far have I travelled in my quest to rid my land of the Skarg. To its furthest corners have I journeyed. Never before have I found a place that is free of them. What is this wondrous haven?

ALEX: Alnwick. [*Or substitute name of the place where the show is being performed.*]

WARRIOR: Alnwick?

ALEX: This is Earth. And, well, the thing is… How can I put this? You are not in your own land any more. Earth is – a different world.

WARRIOR: Ah. A new level. How was I transported here?

ALEX: Good question.

WARRIOR: Only the most powerful alchemy could do such a thing. You must take me to him.

ALEX: Who?

WARRIOR: The great wizard who brought me here. More powerful than a Drathlord must he be. He could help me in my fight against the Skarg. Long have I wished to meet such a man.

CAT: Backwards he's talking, silly twit.
Him and Yoda, think of it.

WARRIOR gives CAT a sharp look and grips his sword.

WARRIOR: What language does that creature speak?

ALEX: She's a cat. She doesn't speak. She just miaows.

WARRIOR: (*Still watching CAT suspiciously.*) Are you sure? It seems to mock me…

CAT gives WARRIOR a Cheshire Cat smile.

Well. No matter. Take me to the powerful one who can open a portal between worlds.

ALEX: Um. That would be me.

He squirms as the WARRIOR stares at him in astonishment.

I don't even know how I did it.

CAT: You made a wish, you silly fool!
Every kitten knows the rule.
Make a wish on Christmas Eve
And it comes true, if you believe.

WARRIOR: Such power in one so young. Truly, you are a great wizard, boy-child.

The WARRIOR goes down on one knee and bows his head.

CAT: Oh, please! Stand up. You can't be happy
Trying to bend down in that nappy.

The WARRIOR surges to his feet and draws his sword. CAT hides behind ALEX.

WARRIOR: I swear that creature is mocking me! I do not know what it is saying but, by the five moons of my land, I will defend my honour!

ALEX: Stop!

ALEX holds out his hand in a blocking gesture. To his surprise, the WARRIOR obeys. From now on, the WARRIOR reacts to CAT's asides with nothing more than a suspicious glare.

OK. Good. Now, can you put that sword away?

The WARRIOR looks down at his sword, then gives ALEX a puzzled look.

CAT: You can't whip out a great big weapon
Every time you're feeling threatened.
Not here. You'll get arrested, see?
This world is real, not fantasy.

ALEX: (*Pointing at the sword.*) Please?

The WARRIOR sheathes his sword.

WARRIOR: (*To ALEX.*) I am the Warrior. If you do not want my sword, why did you call on me, boy-child?

ALEX: My name is Alex, OK?

WARRIOR: (*Imitating ALEX's pronunciation.*) Alex, OK? That is a fine name. Why did you call upon the Warrior, Alex, OK?

ALEX: It seemed like a good idea at the time.

WARRIOR: If you are in need, I will help. That is what I do. What troubles you?

ALEX: It's my Grandad. He's in hospital.

WARRIOR: Maigran D'ad? Is this the name of one of your people?

ALEX: Yes. He's one of my people.

WARRIOR: And what is 'hospital'? The stronghold of your enemy?

ALEX: You could say that. They're going to keep my Grandad in there over Christmas and I really want him home.

WARRIOR: Then let us go to this – hospital.

ALEX: Why?

WARRIOR: To rescue Maigran D'ad.

ALEX: He's not your Grandad. He's my Grandad.

WARRIOR: That is what I said. Maigran D'ad. It is a good name.

ALEX: No, that's not his name... Oh, never mind.

WARRIOR: We must rescue Maigran D'ad from this – hospital.

ALEX: Rescue him? Um, I'm not really sure –

WARRIOR: Maigran D'ad is one of your people?

ALEX: Yes, but...

WARRIOR: And you say this hospital is a bad place?

ALEX: I hate it, but –

WARRIOR: Then let us go. There is no time to lose.

He begins to walk off, then returns and looks at ALEX.

You must lead the way.

ALEX hesitates, then begins getting ready to go out, picking up his scarf and hat.

CAT: But we can't take him out with us
He's wearing tiny, leather knickers!

WARRIOR: (*Watching ALEX collect his outdoor gear then looking down at himself.*) Wait, Alex. Should I don a disguise more in keeping with the garb of your people?

ALEX: Pardon?

WARRIOR: My clothing...

ALEX: You won't look out of place at all tonight.

CAT: Oh, come on Alex! Are you thick?
He'll cause a riot in that kit.

ALEX: (*To WARRIOR.*) It's Christmas Eve. There's a fancy dress parade through town. There'll be loads of people running around in strange gear. They'll think you're a character out of Lord of the Rings or something.

CAT: The Village People is more his style.
All he needs is a hard hat and a smile.

ALEX: (*Stopping and looking down at the scarf and hat in his hands.*) It is cold out there, though. Cold enough to snow.

WARRIOR: Snow?

ALEX: Frozen water. It falls out of the sky in bits.

WARRIOR ducks, holding his shield over his head.

Little white flakes.

ALEX picks up the snowstorm, shakes it and holds it out.

See? Snow.

All three of them watch the swirling snowscene inside the little glass globe.

WARRIOR: Such craftsmanship! What are they doing, the man and the boy?

ALEX: Making a snowman.

WARRIOR: Is this snowman a weapon?

ALEX: No.

WARRIOR: A defensive trick then, to make their army look bigger than it is?

ALEX: No!

WARRIOR: Then why did they build it?

ALEX: For fun! Just for fun.

WARRIOR: Forfun?

ALEX: You know. Fun. Having a good time. A laugh.

ALEX smiles at the WARRIOR who studies his face seriously, then attempts to copy him by stretching his lips in a humourless rictus of a grin. CAT shudders at the sight. ALEX shakes his head, then returns to studying the snowstorm.

They're happy, the man and the boy. They're having fun, building the snowman. See?

He holds out the snowstorm and the WARRIOR takes it. As he looks at the snowstorm, the memory snow music starts, soft and slow. ALEX and the actors playing the two Skarg recreate the snowman-building scene with the parachute silk. One of the SKARG plays ALEX's Dad, in hat and scarf. The other plays the snowman. CAT watches but WARRIOR continues to stare into the snowstorm. Once the snowman is built, ALEX and his Dad stand on either side of it, smiling proudly. Then ALEX's father leaves the stage, dropping his hat and scarf as he goes. The smile leaves ALEX's face and is replaced with a desolate expression. ALEX picks up the hat and scarf, folds them carefully and stares down at them as the snowman melts away. The memory music stops.

So, when I say it's cold enough to snow, I mean it's going to be freezing out there tonight. You won't know what that means because your land is all scorching desert.

WARRIOR: How do you have such knowledge of my land? Have you travelled there?

ALEX: Oh, yes. Many times. Well, not exactly travelled. I can watch you – (*Pointing at the screen.*) – through that – that portal there. Anyway, the point is, you'll freeze if you go out like that.

WARRIOR looks uncomprehendingly at ALEX who does an impression of being cold.

You'll be cold. The trouble is I don't think I have anything to fit you. Mum cleared out all dad's clothes last year. But I have a scarf and a hat you could wear!

ALEX holds out his dad's hat and scarf. The WARRIOR refuses them, striking a noble pose.

WARRIOR: The Warrior feels no cold.

ALEX: (*Putting on his own scarf and hat.*) Suit yourself. Let's go.

ALEX tries to take the snowstorm from the WARRIOR, but he resists.

WARRIOR: May I carry this talisman on our quest?

ALEX hesitates then nods agreement.

ALEX: All right. But please, look after it.

The WARRIOR stows the snowstorm carefully in his belt pouch, then follows ALEX and CAT outside (Sound FX howling wind). As the cold air hits him, the WARRIOR brings his knees together, wraps his arms around his torso and gives a high, girly scream. ALEX and CAT both turn to see what the noise is about. Hastily, WARRIOR straightens. They turn away again and he follows them off-stage, hunched and shivering.

Scene 6

SKARG 1, SKARG 2

Back in ALEX's bedroom, all is still for a few seconds, then the SKARG music/sound effects start to play as two black shapes rise up and step out through the screen. The SKARG have followed the WARRIOR out of the game. They move around the space, still in insect form, sniffing out the WARRIOR's trail. They make insect-like noises – clicks and hisses. Satisfied that their enemy is here in this world, they begin to mutate, becoming an approximation of human.

The change is an awkward, jerky, even painful process and, once they have become sort of human, they do not look quite comfortable with it. Their movements are unnatural. Their speech rhythms and mannerisms could be slightly off-key or interspersed with insect-like clicks.

SKARG 1: So. This is Earth. And we must be – human.

Looks down at himself, then at SKARG 2.

What ugly, awkward bodies they have.

SKARG 2: Nd-a-chhhh-lak-lak-ishka!

SKARG 1: Speak to me in human.

SKARG 2 tries again but still comes out with SKARG.

Speak human! That is an order!

SKARG 2 hits the side of her head.

SKARG 2: I make apologies, my leader. My translation chip is fault-eeeeeeeee!

SKARG 2's high pitched squeal stops as she smacks the side of her head again.

Again, I make apologies, my lee-ee-ee-ee-(*Smack.*)-der. There is trouble with my volume control also.

SKARG 1: Pay attention! The Warrior is here, in this world. I can smell him. We must keep our human form in order to track him without drawing attention to ourselves.

SKARG 2: Eat my shorts!

A horrified SKARG 2 claps her hands over her mouth.

SKARG 1: What did you say!

SKARG 2: Apologies, Sir. I am now picking up interference from something called (*In an American accent.*) Sky Movies.

SKARG 1: I am warning you, Private Nee-sta-ch-ch-pik –

SKARG 2: Do you feel lucky? Well, do you, punk?

SKARG 2 claps a hand over her mouth.

Once again, my apolog–

SKARG 1: Shut up! As soon as we return to our world I'm putting you on a charge.

SKARG 2: Don't make me angry. You won't like me when I'm angry.

SKARG 1: I don't like you very much now, Private!

SKARG 2: (*Coming to attention.*) Sir!

SKARG 1: Now, as I was saying, we must try not to draw attention to ourselves –

SKARG 2: Screeeeeeee–! (*Smack.*)

SKARG 1: – So we must not use our real names. They sound too alien to the human ear. We must each choose a name more suited to this world.

SKARG 2: Yes Sir! I shall be called –

She hurries to the front of the space, eager to redeem herself, and looks out.

Bus stop!

SKARG 1: Bus stop?

SKARG 2: See. It is written on that sign out there.

SKARG 1: Bus stop. Good. I shall be called –

SKARG 2: (*Pointing eagerly.*) Taxi Rank?

SKARG 1: (*Gives SKARG 2 a withering glance then looks outside again.*) No. I shall be called No Ball Games Please.

SKARG 2: Sir, forgive me, but that name is too long for me to remember.

SKARG 1: Oh, for goodness – Very well. I shall be called… Dorothy Perkins!

He strikes a macho pose but SKARG 2 looks doubtful.

SKARG 2: Maybe not…

SKARG 1: Oh, very well!

He looks around ALEX's room and picks up an aerosol deodorant.

I shall be called, Sure for Men.

He sprays under his arms and then into SKARG 2's face.

SKARG 2: (*Spluttering.*) Sure for Men. That is a noble name. And Sure is very much like Sir! Yes. I shall remember that name.

SKARG 1: Now, let us go hunting, while the trail is still f-f-f-f-fresh.

SKARG 2: Again, Sure, f-f-f-forgive me, but is that wise?

SKARG 1: Explain yourself, Bus Stop.

SKARG 2: Very well, Sure for Men. I was thinking –

Thoughtful, moving around the space. She picks up ALEX's games handset.

– the human who brought the Warrior here was able to open a portal between our worlds.

SKARG 1: Go on.

SKARG 2 begins to press the buttons. Behind her, SKARG 1 suddenly finds that his arm is shooting in and out uncontrollably, in time with the clicks of the handset buttons. SKARG 2 stops and SKARG 1 stares down at his arm in puzzlement. SKARG 2 continues pressing buttons and SKARG 1goes into a 'dance' routine made up of jumps, rolls, side steps etc, dictated by the particular button SKARG 2 is pressing. His face is furious but he cannot speak – or stop. A couple of times he may get close enough to reach out his hands and prepare to strangle the unwitting SKARG 2, but always the handset sends him off in another direction at the last second. SKARG 2 talks on, unaware of what is happening behind her.

SKARG 2: He must be a very powerful wizard. Even these artefacts scattered carelessly around his dwelling are beyond our understanding. I think it would be dangerous to follow him openly, even in human disguise. But my sensors detect a network of underground passages, and there is a portal leading down to the passages, over here.

SKARG 2 throws the handset down and goes to the back of the space, still not realising what has been happening to SKARG 1. Behind her, he bends over, panting, trying to recover himself before she turns back to him.

This is the portal. I believe it is called a 'loo'. The underground passageways are called sew-ers.

Turning back to SKARG 1, she stops and stares in puzzlement

Are you well, Sure?

SKARG 1 waves her on, wordlessly.

To pass through this portal-loo – we must become smaller. I detect many rodents in the sewers. I believe the common term for them in this world is 'rats'.

They both imitate the squeaking of a rat.

SKARG 1: So. If we take on the form of these 'rats', we can pass through the portal-loo and follow our enemy undetected. Good thinking Bus Stop. After you.

SKARG 2 beams with pride, then goes about becoming a rat. SKARG 1 picks up the games handset, looks at it thoughtfully, then hides it in his belt pouch before also shape-shifting into the form of a rat. They both disappear to the Sound FX of a flushing toilet.

Scene 7

ALEX, WARRIOR, CAT

ALEX, WARRIOR and CAT enter.

WARRIOR: Why is the talisman precious to you?

ALEX: My Dad gave it to me.

WARRIOR: MaiD'ad? Is this another of your people?

ALEX: We used to build snowmen together. See?

He points to the figures in the snowstorm.

Me and my Dad. The snowstorm reminds me of him.

WARRIOR: Why do you need reminding of this MaiD'ad?

ALEX: He died.

CAT snuggles against ALEX's side, wordlessly comforting him. ALEX strokes her.

WARRIOR: He will return when New Game begins.

ALEX: No. I told you. He died.

WARRIOR: But those who die always return – in New Game.

ALEX: Not here. We don't have New Game here.

WARRIOR: No New Game?

ALEX: No. In this world, when someone gets too hurt or too sick, that's it. Game Over.

WARRIOR: What is hurt?

ALEX: You know. Injured. Um… Pain?

WARRIOR: (*Striking a pose.*) The Warrior feels no pain.

ALEX: Maybe not in your world. But things are different in this world.

WARRIOR: The Warrior feels no pain wherever he is.

CAT: These claws are sharp and very long.
I would so love to prove him wrong.

WARRIOR: Watch. I will demonstrate. No pain.

Swaggering, the WARRIOR draws his sword and holds the blade over his open palm. Smiling, he looks at ALEX as he draws the blade across his palm. His smile disappears. He flinches and drops the sword.

Owww…!

The WARRIOR stares at his palm where the blood is beginning to flow, then he staggers back and forth until, finally, he falls backwards. ALEX and CAT just manage to catch him. CAT sinks further and further down under his weight.

CAT: 'The Warrior feels no pain,' my paw!
I ought to drop him on the floor.
He's as wobbly as a jelly
A hero? Him? Not on your nellie.

CAT and ALEX sit WARRIOR down.

WARRIOR: (*Coming round again and holding out his hand.*)
I am leaking!

CAT: 'Oh, I'm leaking…' What a sissie.
He's nothing but a great big jessie.

ALEX: (*Producing a handkerchief and wrapping it around the WARRIOR's hand.*) It's only blood.

WARRIOR: Blood? This does not happen in my world.

ALEX: Don't worry. It isn't deep.

WARRIOR: Your world is a dreadful place, with the pain and the dying and no New Game.

ALEX: It's not that bad.

The WARRIOR gets to his feet and begins to exit.

WARRIOR: We must return to your dwelling now! We will be safe there.

ALEX: I thought we were going to the hospital?

WARRIOR: (*Stopping and turning.*) But, look! (*Holding out his hand.*) How do you find the courage to step out into this world every day?

ALEX: Well, you learn.

WARRIOR: What do you 'learn'?

ALEX: The rules, I suppose.

WARRIOR: Ah! There are rules!

CAT: Don't cut yourself on purpose is Rule One.
Rule two, it isn't clever to be strong.
Rule Three, a daily shower would be nice.
That smell's enough to put me off my mice.

ALEX: Well, not rules, exactly. You just learn how to take care of yourself. And people look out for one another, mostly. If we hid away inside our houses all the time, there'd be no point in being alive, would there?

WARRIOR: Why not?

ALEX: Because we'd miss out on all the good stuff.

WARRIOR: Good stuff?

ALEX: See over there? That's the shopping centre. On Christmas Eve, it's a magical place. Look! I can see the carol singers by the entrance! They're there every year. Me and my Grandad always join in with the singing.

WARRIOR: What is this – singing?

ALEX: You'll find out. Come on! You'll love it!

ALEX and CAT hurry off-stage. WARRIOR very carefully picks up his sword and puts it back into its sheath, hissing with anxiety.

WARRIOR: Careful! Sharp. Very sharp.

Then, also very carefully, he follows ALEX and CAT, stepping slowly and shying away from passers-by.

Careful. Don't walk so fast. Get away from me!

Scene 8

SKARG 1, SKARG 2, ALEX, CAT, WARRIOR

As the WARRIOR exits, SKARGS 1 and 2 scramble on-stage through the screen, accompanied by the sound of angry rats squealing. They are both batting at their clothes and hitting at something off-stage.

SKARG 2: (*In Sky Movie mode.*) You dirty rat…

SKARG 1: Close the portal! Close it!

Hastily, SKARG 2 slams down the off-stage manhole cover (or, if using a raised stage, a trapdoor could be utilised) and they both take a minute to recover themselves, straightening their clothes, brushing themselves down.

SKARG 2: Well! Those rodents weren't very friendly, were they Sure?

SKARG 1: Not very friendly? Not very friendly? I would rather face a herd of rampaging slimebeasts! Nip, nip, squeak, squeak, nibble, nibble all the way! I'm staying in human form from now on.

SKARG 2: But my plan worked, Sir. I mean, Sure. We have tracked the Warrior to this…shop-ping cent-ur…without being detected.

SKARG 1: We shall merge into the crowd and wait until our enemy is separated from the young wizard. Once there is no magic to protect the Warrior, we will take our chance.

The SKARG take out hats and scarves and hastily put them on as, on the other side of the space, the carol singers (could be lifesize 'glove' puppets) appear, accompanied (or carried) by ALEX, CAT and WARRIOR. The two SKARG merge into the group and join in singing 'In the Bleak Mid-Winter' in unaccompanied harmony. To start with, the WARRIOR is edgy and anxious to avoid any contact that might lead to pain, but, as he hears beautiful music for the first time, he becomes totally involved in the singing. In a transformational moment, candles appear in the hands of the singers, the Christmas tree lights shine out and there is a suggestion of glittering frost or snow all around. The carol finishes and there is a moment of silence before WARRIOR, CAT and ALEX step away from the carol singers (if using puppets, handing them over to the SKARG). The SKARG and carol singers then continue to hum the tune softly.

WARRIOR: I – There is a strange feeling here, in my chest. Soft… Warm…

CAT: Heartburn. Take some Gaviscon.

ALEX: (*To WARRIOR.*) See. I told you. Good stuff.

WARRIOR: What will they sing next?

ALEX: I'll ask them.

He turns to SKARG 1 and 2. They freeze in place.

Excuse me.

Instantly, the humming stops. The two SKARG do a 'Me...? Him...? Me....?' routine, pointing at themselves, the other singers and one another.

What are you singing next?

SKARG 1: Go on, Bus Stop!

SKARG 2: Me?

SKARG 1: Yes, you. The wizard commands you to sing. So sing!

SKARG 2 gives SKARG 1 a desperate look and then turns back to ALEX. She clears her throat and opens her mouth. She has no idea what is going to come out.

SKARG 2: (*As Marilyn.*)
'H... Ha... Happy Birthday, Mr President
Happy Birthday to you
A diddly diddly diddly dum, booboobeedoo –
eeeeeeeeee!'

SKARG 2 claps a hand over her mouth, cutting short the high-pitched shriek that she is suddenly emitting. An intrigued CAT begins to sniff at the SKARG.

ALEX: Well, I guess that must be it with the carols for a while.

WARRIOR: No more of the singing?

ALEX: Not here. They're, um, taking a break. (*An idea hits him.*) But if you want to sing, I know just where to take you!

CAT: (*Still sniffing.*) It's strange. We're nowhere near a loo
But these two really smell of –

ALEX: Snowball! Come on, cat!

WARRIOR: Where are we going?

ALEX: Up the escalator to the Kara-oke Kafe!

Scene 9

ALEX, CAT, WARRIOR, SKARG 1, SKARG 2

Christmas musak (such as Wizard's 'Let the Bells Ring Out for Christmas') begins to play as they reach the bottom of the escalator. The WARRIOR is still wary of anything which might hurt him in this world and is unsure of the moving steps. The following scene can all be created with physical theatre. As the SKARG watch, ALEX works to persuade WARRIOR onto the escalator.

ALEX: Come on, Warrior! It's easy! It's only an escalator. Just step on and grab the handrail!

WARRIOR tries, but his courage fails him and he steps back again.

Come on! You can do it! (*Demonstrating.*) Step and grab! Step – and grab.

CAT: Two things at once? I don't think so. His brain's too small to cope, you know.

CAT gives WARRIOR a push and all three of them begin to ride the up escalator. The SKARG are watching with interest. At the top, the WARRIOR turns and immediately steps onto the down escalator with a broad grin on his face.

WARRIOR: Forfun!

The SKARG are by now riding on the up escalator, passing the WARRIOR mid-way. This farce continues, using the screen as a side view of the escalators, until WARRIOR, CAT and ALEX step through the screen and off-stage. Meanwhile the two SKARG end up in a heap at the bottom of the escalator.

SKARG 1: That was a disaster. The Warrior is too strong for us to tackle in our human form, yet we dare not become Skarg in such a public place.

SKARG 2: And we cannot confront the boy wizard. His powers are too great. Did you see how he made the steps move?

SKARG 1: But, there is a third companion.

SKARG 2: The white-haired creature that journeys with them.

SKARG 1: Access your data banks, Bus Stop, and download all information about this creature.

SKARG 2 frowns with concentration, then begins to sing, jumping from one song fragment to another. 'Memories', 'Cool for Cats', 'Everybody Wants to Be a Cat', 'What's New, Pussycat?' etc. SKARG 1 waits impatiently for her to finish.

SKARG 2: The creature is a small mammal known as – a cat! She is not strong. She has no magic.

SKARG 1: And the boy is very fond of her. If we could capture the cat creature –

SKARG 2: – then we would have power over the boy wizard!

SKARG 1: Good. That is our new mission. We will shadow them until the cat is unprotected.

SKARG 2: – and then we will capture it.

The two SKARG hurry off, delighted with their new plan. Meanwhile…

Scene 10

ALEX, CAT, WARRIOR, SKARG 1, SKARG 2

...the frame at the back of the space has now become a stage in the Kara-oke Kafe. The WARRIOR is standing with his back to the audience, in an instantly recognisable Elvis pose. ALEX and CAT stand on either side of the frame. They will become backing singers. The introductory music to 'It'll Be Lonely this Christmas' (or similar) starts up. The WARRIOR turns, moves out into the main space and begins his performance, complete with Elvis movements. He has a mic in his hand and he is wearing Elvis shades and cuffs. The SKARG each work their way around opposite sides of the space, clicking their fingers. They disappear around the sides of the screen and emerge in the screen, also becoming backing singers, moving to the beat and oooh-aaahhing until the song ends. Applause.

WARRIOR: (*Still Elvis.*) Thank you very much.

ALEX: That was brilliant!

WARRIOR: (*Himself again. Elvis has left the building.*) I am
    beginning to enjoy this level.

CAT: Oh, dear. Our friend in leather gear
    Is getting rather comfy here.
    He thinks he's starting to belong
    Just because he sang a song.
    And Alex seems to like him. See?
    Of course, that doesn't bother me!

WARRIOR: Now it is your turn, Alex!

ALEX: No thanks. I don't really sing.

WARRIOR: Why not? Singing is wonderful!

ALEX: I'm no good at it. I can't belt them out like you can.

CAT: Don't tell him that! He'll get ideas.
    I'd rather stick pins in my ears

Than let him have another go.

Besides, you sing quite well, you know.

Compared to me, you're pretty grotty.

Compared with him, you're Pavarotti.

WARRIOR: Quickly, Alex! The next song is starting!

WARRIOR pushes the mic into ALEX's hand. ALEX reluctantly begins to sing 'White Christmas' (or a similar Christmas song). WARRIOR and CAT join in and the SKARG again provide backing vocals. ALEX is shuffling, embarrassed. WARRIOR keeps making encouraging hand gestures as he removes his Elvis shades and cuffs. At some point in the song, WARRIOR comes up beside ALEX and helps him with the song. Then, WARRIOR can't resist taking over, pulling the mic out of ALEX's hand and giving him a shove to the side as he takes centre stage. ALEX stops singing and finds somewhere to sit down. We see that he is upset. The WARRIOR carries on for a few more bars, then sees ALEX and stops singing. Behind him, the SKARG continue to sing backing vocals sotto voce.

Alex?

ALEX has his head down and does not answer but the WARRIOR sees that he is crying.

Now you are leaking!

ALEX wipes his face.

Why are you sad, Alex?

ALEX: That was my dad's favourite song.

WARRIOR: This MaiD'ad must have been very special to you.

ALEX: He was my father!

WARRIOR: Father?

CAT: He won't know what father means.
  He's built from microchips, not genes.
  He doesn't know how sad you feel.
  Don't get too close. He isn't real.

ALEX: You must have had a father.

WARRIOR: No.

ALEX: But – a father and a mother – they're part of who you are.

WARRIOR: I know who I am. I am the Warrior.

ALEX: But, weren't you ever a boy like me?

WARRIOR: I am the Warrior. I was always the Warrior.

ALEX: So you have no family?

WARRIOR: I am the Warrior! I need no family! I need no father!

Pause.

What is – a father?

ALEX: Well, I can tell you about my father. He sang nearly as badly as you do. And his dancing was even worse. He was a real embarrassment at parties. What else? He taught me how to ride a bike. I remember him running beside me, holding onto the saddle until I was ready to set off on my own. He was always there beside me, holding onto the saddle.

WARRIOR: What is a bike? Is it a weapon?

ALEX: No.

WARRIOR: A defensive trick then –

ALEX: No! Forget the bike. My Dad… He was… I was…

CAT: They were two halves of the same thing.

Linked by blood. The closest kin.
But you're too dim to understand.
Why don't you go back to your land!

The WARRIOR is still looking mystified. ALEX tries again.

ALEX: He looked after me. Kept me safe. He was my
shield. He was my sword.

The WARRIOR nods, finally understanding.

WARRIOR: Your protector.

ALEX: I scored two brilliant goals last week. We won the
match. I really wanted to tell him about it. Mum said,
maybe he knew. Do you think he knew?

WARRIOR shrugs.

WARRIOR: I cannot answer that.

*ALEX turns away and WARRIOR rests a hand on his shoulder.
ALEX turns back and hugs him fiercely. WARRIOR stands
for a moment with his arms wide, then he brings his arms
around the boy and, awkwardly, pats him on the back. They
are silent for a space. CAT, hurt and excluded, walks away
from them. She stands in front of the SKARG, watching
ALEX.*

*Suddenly, the SKARG stop singing backing vocals. SKARG
1 begins to stroke CAT's head.*

SKARG 1: Now…

SKARG 2: (*Drowsily.*) What?

SKARG 1: Now!

*SKARG 2 produces a sack made out of stretchy material.
They leap out of the frame and pull the sack down over CAT.
CAT miaows in panic.*

ALEX: Snowball!

ALEX grabs the sack and he and SKARG 2 have a tug of war with the sack as SKARG 2 attempts to drag CAT off-stage. Meanwhile, SKARG 1 turns to the WARRIOR, pulling the games handset from his belt pouch as he does so. He points the handset at the WARRIOR. The WARRIOR rushes forward, drawing his sword, but the handset freezes him on pause with the sword held above his head. Throughout the rest of this scene, the WARRIOR struggles to break out of his paralysis, but cannot. ALEX continues to struggle to save CAT but is losing the battle.

What are you doing?

SKARG 2: We are...

SKARG 2 accesses her data banks.

We are... Evening all... Alpha, Bravo, Charlie, Delta... Yes! That's it! We are police officers. This is a suspected cat burglar. We are taking it in for questioning.

ALEX: You're not police! You're those two mad carol singers. Let her go! She's mine!

ALEX loses his grip on the sack and falls onto his back. SKARG 2 heads off-stage with CAT, turning just before she disappears.

SKARG 2: Hasta la vista, baby!

ALEX: Snowball!

SKARG 1 sees that SKARG 2 has successfully kidnapped CAT. He throws down the games handset and makes a run for it, leaping over ALEX's prone body and exiting after SKARG 2. WARRIOR comes out of his paralysis as ALEX clambers to his feet and turns to face him.

I thought you were a hero! Why didn't you help me?

WARRIOR: I – could not move –

ALEX: You're nothing but a big coward!

ALEX exits, running.

WARRIOR: Alex, wait.

WARRIOR watches ALEX exit, then bends and picks up the games handset. He sniffs at the handset. Realisation dawns.

Skarg....

WARRIOR draws his sword and exits, following ALEX, to the hero music.

End of Act One.

ACT TWO

Scene 1

CAT, SKARG 1, SKARG 2, ALEX, WARRIOR

ALEX runs on, followed by WARRIOR, still carrying the games handset.

ALEX: Snowball! Where are you?

ALEX searches the space. He is desperately upset. Meanwhile, the WARRIOR has spotted something. He walks over and stares down into the dark entrance to a stormdrain.

They came this way, I'm sure of it. They can't just disappear into thin air.

WARRIOR: They have taken the creature underground.

ALEX: Don't call her that! She's not just a creature! She's my cat!

WARRIOR raises his hands in acknowledgement and steps back as ALEX rushes over to the trapdoor.

(*To himself.*) It's a storm drain. Big enough to walk along.

ALEX hesitates for a moment – it is very dark down there – then he prepares to descend into the storm drain. WARRIOR grabs his arm to stop him.

WARRIOR: Wait. There is great danger down there.

ALEX: (*Shaking him off.*) Don't you touch me! I thought you were a hero. I thought you were my friend.

WARRIOR: I am –

ALEX: No you're not! It's easy to be brave in your world, where nothing hurts and nobody dies. In my world a hero is someone who does the right thing, even if they're really scared. You're not a hero at all.

WARRIOR: I meant – I am your friend.

ALEX: Oh. Well – you're not that either. Friends are supposed to stick together. You just stood back and watched!

WARRIOR: I could not move.

ALEX: Because you were too scared –

WARRIOR: No. (*He holds out the handset.*) Because of this.

ALEX takes the handset.

It is one of your magical devices, is it not? It is broken now, but when it was still whole, the Skarg used its magic to freeze me in place.

ALEX: It's my handset. He must've put you on pause…

WARRIOR: I was trying to reach you, Alex. I was trying so hard, but I could not move. I am sorry. I failed you.

WARRIOR bows his head. A pause.

ALEX: Well, don't just stand there like a wet lettuce.

WARRIOR raises his head.

We have to rescue Snowball.

WARRIOR: We?

ALEX: I told you. Friends always stick together. Let's go.

WARRIOR: Wait.

ALEX: What now?

WARRIOR: You do not understand the danger.

ALEX: Danger? From those two? I don't think so. They're a bit pathetic, really. We could take them, me and you.

ALEX makes some martial arts-type fighting moves but slowly comes to an embarrassed halt when WARRIOR simply stares at him.

WARRIOR: Why do you think they captured the creature?

ALEX: Snowball's a pedigree cat. They could make quite a bit of money if they found a buyer for her.

WARRIOR: No. They are setting a trap.

ALEX: A trap?

WARRIOR: For me.

ALEX: That's just stupid.

WARRIOR: You do not understand. They are not what they seem. They are not human.

ALEX: What are they?

WARRIOR: Skarg.

Involuntarily, ALEX steps away from the dark hole as a harsh sigh rises from it.

They must have followed me through the portal into this world. You are right. In their human form, they are not strong yet. But down there, in the dark, where no-one can see them, they do not need to stay in human form. They will change. They will become Skarg.

Another harsh sigh from the darkness.

Do you know what that means, Alex? They are strong. Much stronger than us. They have fangs and claws that carry a poison so powerful, one bite – one scratch – will kill you. And they can see in the dark.

ALEX: I – I don't like the dark. Not really. But they've got Snowball. I'm going down there.

He goes to the trapdoor, hesitates.

And you can't stop me.

WARRIOR: I do not wish to stop you.

ALEX: Oh.

WARRIOR: But we cannot go into the dark unprepared. We must find some source of light.

ALEX looks around.

ALEX: There's an electrical store. I'll nip in and buy a couple of torches. You wait for me over by that big television.

WARRIOR: Television?

ALEX: That big screen over there at the front of the shop. (*He points to the frame.*) I'll be as fast as I can.

ALEX exits and WARRIOR goes to stand by the frame.

Scene 2

ALEX, WARRIOR, THREE 'ER' CAST MEMBERS

WARRIOR inspects the television and then jumps back in shock as the theme tune to 'ER' blasts out. He kneels to watch the television as three green-gowned and masked figures appear in the frame. We hear the bleep of a heart monitor.

DOC 1: (*Talking extremely quickly in an American accent.*) We have to move fast. He had a DVD in HMV. He's forgotten his ABC and his MPH is down to zero.

DOC 2: We have to intubate.

DOC 3 produces a length of extremely springy rubber hosing and proceeds to 'fight' with it in the background.

DOC 1: (*Examining the body.*) Oh, no.

DOC 2: What is it?

DOC 1: He has no GCSEs!

DOC 2: What are his SATs scores?

DOC 1: Very low. But he does have an HGV –

DOC 2: That won't help him now.

DOC 1: We could give him GBH.

DOC 2: It's too late for that. Scalpel!

DOC 3 gives up on the tubing and hands DOC 2 a cut-throat razor. The beep of the heart monitor becomes one, drawn out note.

DOC 1: He's going into V-Tec! Shock him.

DOC 3 looks from the body to DOC 1 to DOC 2 to the body.

I said, shock him!

DOC 3 leans over the body, makes his hands into monster claws and growls ferociously/shouts 'boo'.

DOC 2: Will somebody get that med student out of here!

DOC 1 pushes DOC 3 out of the way and grabs the paddles.

DOC 1: Clear!

DOC 1 administers the shock. The heart monitor begins to beep again.

DOC 2: Well done guys. We saved another life today.

DOC 1: That's what hospitals are for. Saving lives.

'ER' music swells again as the figures pose heroically before leaving the screen. WARRIOR stands again, looking thoughtful.

WARRIOR: Saving lives…?

ALEX returns, carrying two torches.

ALEX: Ready?

WARRIOR: Alex, this place where Maigran D'ad is being held.

ALEX: The hospital?

WARRIOR: Yes. Hospital. Why was he taken there?

ALEX: He got sick.

WARRIOR: And is he getting worse, in hospital?

ALEX: No. He's getting better.

WARRIOR: Then why do you wish to take him out of there?

ALEX: Hospitals are bad places.

WARRIOR: But I have just seen a hospital on the tele-vis-ion. They saved a man's life. They were helping him.

ALEX: Yeah, right! That's what Mum said when my Dad went into hospital. But he died there. I hate hospitals!

WARRIOR: But, what if he was too sick to be helped, even though they tried their best?

ALEX refuses to answer WARRIOR.

Maybe Maigran D'ad is better off where he is –

ALEX: I don't have time to talk about this now. I have to rescue Snowball. Are you coming or not?

WARRIOR: Of course I am.

ALEX moves towards the stormdrain, but WARRIOR holds him back.

I will go first. It is dangerous down there. You could be hurt.

ALEX: In this world, so could you.

WARRIOR: I will go first.

WARRIOR goes into the stormdrain first. ALEX follows.

Scene 3

CAT, SKARG 1, SKARG 2

The stage darkens. A hollow, echo-ey dripping can be heard. We are at the far end of the storm drain. The frame at the back of the stage is now the end of the tunnel, the way to the outside world. The two SKARG enter, dragging CAT between them. They are still in human form and somewhat out of breath. They leave CAT centre-stage and check out the space.

SKARG 2: (*Inspecting the frame.*) This is the end of the tunnel. Beyond the opening is the outside world.

SKARG 1: Then this is where we must set our trap.

SKARG 2: Will the trap work?

SKARG 1: They will come for this bait, I am sure of it.

SKARG 2: Then we should become Skarg…

SKARG 1: Not yet. First I wish to find out what I can from this creature.

SKARG 2: So. Let us become cats.

The two SKARG transform into cats, and then come to stand on either side of CAT, pulling the sack off her and placing it on the floor in front of her as they do so. CAT is frightened but puts on a brave face, giving each of them a disdainful look before starting to groom herself. They copy her movements precisely.

CAT: So, you're Skarg. I should have guessed.
You move like drunken marionettes.
And your singing was unlawful.
Even humans aren't that awful!
And now you're cats? Don't make me laugh.
Your whiskers droop, your fur is naff.

(*To SKARG 1.*) Oh, that colour. So last season!
(*To SKARG 2.*) And that cut. Was there a reason?

The SKARG look offended and uncomfortable, particularly SKARG 2, who – influenced by Sky Movies – is beginning to harbour dreams of becoming a Hollywood star. Smugly, CAT begins to groom herself again. They copy her. CAT begins to set them increasingly athletic challenges. Finally, she grabs her foot and gracefully straightens one leg above her head. Again, they copy her, then both slowly keel over still with their legs outstretched. A beat, then, still lying on their backs, they both groan.

You sound as though you need the vet.
Don't give up your day jobs yet.

The SKARG struggle into a sitting position again.

I'd like to help, but I can't stay.
My Alex will be on his way.

CAT looks hopefully over her shoulder and heads for the frame. The SKARG intercept her.

SKARG 1: Ah, yes, the wizard. Is he strong?

CAT responds in the typically arrogant, thoughtless way we have grown to expect. She talks on, unaware that she is wading deeper into trouble. As they realise what CAT is saying, the SKARG exchange satisfied glances over her head, then clamber to their feet and stand behind her.

CAT: Alex? No, you've got it wrong.
　　He's not a wizard, just a boy.
　　One of the humans I employ.
　　Frankly, they're a waste of time.
　　They can't even speak in rhyme!

Too late, CAT realises what she has done. With the SKARG standing behind her, she tries to climb out of the hole she has just dug.

Did you say Alex? My mistake.
I thought you meant that other fake.
You know, the one in leather gear?
Now Alex, he's the one to fear.
He's very strong. His spells are stunning.
If I were you, I'd exit running.

The SKARG are not taken in. SKARG 2 points to the sack on the floor in front of CAT. With a pathetic miaow, she steps into the sack and SKARG 2 pulls it up and over her head.

SKARG 1: Leave the creature's head free.

SKARG 2: But then it will be able to call for help.

SKARG 1: I know.

SKARG 2: But that will lead them right here.

SKARG 1: I know. This is a trap.

SKARG 2: Ah. Yes.

SKARG 1: You have a tiny, tiny brain, don't you?

SKARG 2: (*Saluting.*) Sure.

SKARG 1: Get on with it!

SKARG 2 adjusts the sack so that CAT's head is sticking out but she is still imprisoned. The two SKARG turn and slowly walk to the back of the space. As they walk, the Skarg music

*starts up and their movements and noises become insect-like.
They are resuming their true shape. CAT watches, becoming
increasingly terrified as she sees what they are becoming. They
reach the back of the space and melt into the shadows of the
tunnel wall. Music stops.*

Scene 4

CAT

*Once the SKARG have disappeared, CAT begins to struggle in the
stretchy lycra sack. She tries three times and each time her movements
are more frantic. The effect is comic but, at the same time, induces
sympathy. She comes to a halt when she realises she cannot escape
from the sack.*

CAT: I'm bundled up inside a sack
　　Which is the worst thing for a cat!
　　I'm not quite sure what they have planned
　　But ponds and drowning spring to mind.
　　Oh, Alex! Come and rescue me!
　　I'm all tied up! I can't get free!
　　No, wait. He has to stay well clear.
　　They'll catch him if he comes too near.
　　So, even though I want to shout
　　I must be silent as a mouse.
　　If I'm quiet, he won't search here.
　　Darkness is his greatest fear.
　　At home, he has to have a light
　　To keep him safe all through the night.
　　'All through the night'…that was the thing
　　His father always sang to him.
　　A lullaby, soft, sweet and slow.
　　So comforting. I need that now.

*CAT sings the first verse of 'All Through the Night',
unaccompanied.*

'Sleep my child and peace attend thee
All through the night.
Guardian angels I will send thee
All through the night.
Soft the drowsy hours are creeping
Hill and dale in slumber sleeping
I my loved one's watch am keeping
All through the night.'

She falters to a stop and looks around fearfully.

Alex's father went away.
It was a shame he couldn't stay.
I don't think he'll be coming back.
Perhaps they put him in a sack.
Oh, it's no good, I must get out!
I'm so scared, I have to shout!
Alex! Help me Alex…!

CAT's voice fades as she moves to the side of the space and curls up, out of sight.

Scene 5

SKARG 1, SKARG 2, CAT, ALEX, WARRIOR

WARRIOR and ALEX enter cautiously, with torches. WARRIOR has his sword unsheathed.

WARRIOR: Wait here. Don't move.

ALEX waits as WARRIOR edges into the centre of the space. ALEX does not like being left behind in the dark tunnel, so he creeps up behind WARRIOR. WARRIOR does not notice – he swings first to the right, then to the left, checking out the space. Behind him, ALEX does the same. When WARRIOR faces forward again, ALEX goes up on tiptoe and whispers in his ear.

ALEX: Can you see anything?

WARRIOR swings round with a startled yell, sword held high. At the last second he stops the downward swing of the weapon.

WARRIOR: Alex! I told you to wait over there!

ALEX: I'm sorry.

WARRIOR: I nearly – You nearly – I told you not to move!

ALEX: I didn't want to be left alone in the dark.

WARRIOR: It might be the safest thing to do.

ALEX: But – I don't like the dark.

WARRIOR: I know. But I do not hunt well with you beside me.

ALEX: I'll be quiet. I'll stay exactly where you put me. I promise.

WARRIOR: That will not stop me being afraid for you. The fear that you might be hurt is distracting me from my task.

ALEX: Don't leave me alone. Please!

WARRIOR: The dark will not hurt you. It is more dangerous for you to stay close to me. I am the one the Skarg are seeking. Perhaps I should go on alone.

ALEX: No! You can't leave me! You might not come back.

WARRIOR: That is true.

ALEX: And in my world it's not just Game Over. It's Game Over and Out. Goodbye!

WARRIOR: Everyone has to say goodbye sometime.

ALEX: He didn't!

WARRIOR: Do you talk of your kinsman, MaiD'ad?

ALEX: One day he was there. The next he was gone.

WARRIOR: Alex, if we stay together, you could be hurt. The Skarg will show no mercy.

ALEX: I don't care. I'd rather face them than stay here alone. If you go away, you might never come back.

WARRIOR: All right. We will stay together.

ALEX: All right.

The WARRIOR prepares himself. ALEX copies. WARRIOR moves off with ALEX shadowing him. ALEX slips his arm through WARRIOR's and clasps his wrist. WARRIOR stops.

WARRIOR: Alex. I said we would stay together.

ALEX: OK.

ALEX removes his arm. WARRIOR prepares himself. ALEX copies and they move on. ALEX slips his arm through WARRIOR's again. WARRIOR stops.

WARRIOR: Alex, I cannot fight with you hanging onto my arm.

ALEX: (*Letting go.*) But you might try and sneak off.

WARRIOR: I won't go anywhere without saying goodbye first.

ALEX: You promise?

WARRIOR: I promise.

ALEX: OK.

WARRIOR prepares himself again. ALEX copies him. They move on. ALEX stays close but this time does not try to hold onto WARRIOR as they move onwards. Then, CAT miaows behind them.

Scene 6

ALEX, WARRIOR, CAT, SKARG 1, SKARG 2

ALEX and the WARRIOR turn and hurry towards the noise.

ALEX: There she is!

> *ALEX runs to CAT. WARRIOR moves more slowly, checking for SKARG. ALEX brings CAT to the front of the space, still in the sack. WARRIOR moves to stand guard behind ALEX and CAT. They do not notice the SKARG detaching themselves from the shadows and slowly creeping up behind them. In human form they may be comical, but as SKARG there is nothing funny about them at all. Scary Skarg music begins.*

> (*Struggling to get the sack off CAT.*) It's all right, Snowball. We'll soon have you out of there.

CAT: (*To ALEX.*) It's so good to see you, dear.
But please be quick. The Skarg are near.
And they've changed. They have such claws,
And dripping fangs and biting jaws.

WARRIOR: Keep the creature quiet, Alex. The Skarg cannot be far away.

CAT: (*To WARRIOR.*) You be quiet, you stupid dolt!
You brought them here. It's all your fault.
How dare you, a virtual stranger,
Bring my Alex into danger?

WARRIOR: Hurry Alex. Hurry!

ALEX: Nearly got it… There!

> *As ALEX finally frees CAT, the SKARG rear up behind them. WARRIOR swings round, placing himself between the SKARG and ALEX.*

WARRIOR: Watch the fangs! Watch the claws! Don't let them touch you!

Fight music plays as the SKARG strike out, attempting to make contact with WARRIOR, ALEX or CAT. WARRIOR counters each strike as ALEX and CAT cower behind him. The SKARG fight as though they are thinking with one brain, co-ordinating their movements and making sudden splitting manoeuvres to attack on two fronts. ALEX uses his torch beam to help when he realises that the SKARG do not like bright lights. During the fight, both ALEX and CAT are isolated and in danger at some stage. Both times, WARRIOR manages to save them, but he is tiring. Finally…

I can't hold them off much longer. The opening behind us. When I say go, run as fast as you can.

The SKARG both strike in unison. WARRIOR holds them back with difficulty. The SKARG snap and lunge at his face. WARRIOR makes a huge effort and pushes the SKARG off-balance so that they stagger back.

Go!

ALEX and CAT leap through the frame (which represents the other end of the storm drain) and exit. The SKARG appear to overwhelm WARRIOR but then he bursts upward again, pushing them off him. As the SKARG fall to the floor, WARRIOR follows ALEX and CAT through the frame. The two SKARG clamber to their feet, changing back into human form as they straighten up. Music ends.

SKARG 1: What is beyond the opening?

SKARG 2: My sensors detect a drop into a pool of deep water. The sides of the pool are steep and smooth. The chances are they will drown in there.

SKARG 1: But we must be sure. We must see the bodies. Come. Let us prepare for an underwater search.

The SKARG exit to one side as…

Scene 7

ALEX, WARRIOR, CAT, SKARG 1, SKARG 2

...in a time-lapse sequence, ALEX, CAT and WARRIOR complete their original leap, still yelling, but this time coming through the frame (i.e. the end of the storm drain) into the space. The lights come up as the three of them land. The instant their feet hit the floor, Skaters' Waltz-type music starts to play. Their yells are cut off, replaced by astonished looks as they all glide across the floor.

ALEX: It's the skating pond! We've come out at the skating pond!

WARRIOR grabs ALEX's arms and they spin round with WARRIOR yelling in fear. The WARRIOR spins off to one side, out of control. ALEX and CAT continue to glide, twirl and spin to the music. ALEX is inexperienced but enthusiastic. WARRIOR returns to the ice as he gets the hang of it. They skate side by side, hands behind their backs as they talk. CAT becomes more and more daring, showing off her skills next to the WARRIOR. She skates back and forth behind the other two as they talk, going one better each time she crosses the space.

WARRIOR: We are safe from them, for now. They cannot come out into the open as Skarg. They must take human form.

ALEX: Thank you, Warrior. You saved us. Didn't he Snowball?

CAT: I hate to say it, but you're right.
He's really useful in a fight.
I don't know how he got us through it.
So, tha...tha...thank... Oh! I can't do it!

CAT flounces off, still gagging over saying 'thank you'.

WARRIOR: Is the creature unwell?

ALEX: Furball.

WARRIOR: I thought it was called Snowball?

CAT pushes them both off the ice and takes over. They stand watching and applauding. They may even hold up scorecards. The skating music stops and WARRIOR looks back to the storm drain exit as he hears something.

Stand back. Here they come.

ALEX, CAT and WARRIOR move to the sides of the space as the two SKARG appear in the frame. They are both wearing brightly coloured snorkels and masks, rubber rings, etc. They hold their noses and jump out onto the ice. They both make swimming motions with their arms but come to a stop as they realise they are standing on slippery ice.

BOTH SKARG: Aaaaaagggggghhhhh!

They collide and fall in a heap.

SKARG 1: Where is the water, Bus Stop?

SKARG 2: (*Struggling to get to her feet and failing miserably.*) My sensors tell me this is water, Sure, but it has undergone some strange transforma-a-a-tion.

Together they try and fail, try and fail, then finally manage to get to their feet. A few, slapstick moments ensue as they attempt to reach ALEX, WARRIOR and CAT but keep shooting off into the audience instead, possibly even hanging onto audience members as they try to find their balance. Finally, they manage to come to a stop in the middle of the space, Bambi-legged and exhausted. SKARG 2 may even jump onto SKARG 1's back to escape from the ice.

SKARG 1: Bus Stop. When we get back, I'm putting you on so many charges –

SKARG 2: But, Sure!

SKARG 1: (*To WARRIOR.*) Do not think you are safe here, Warrior! Every quiet corner – every dark night – we'll be waiting!

SKARG 2: Every move you make, every breath you take, we'll be watching you!

SKARG 1: (*To SKARG 2.*) Plan B.

SKARG 2: Sure?

SKARG 1: Back to the tunnel.

> *They make their wobbly way back to the frame. SKARG 1 stumbles over the lip of the frame but SKARG 2 turns back to WARRIOR.*

SKARG 2: (*As Arnie.*) I'll be back…

> *SKARG 2 grips SKARG 1 by the shoulder in a vulcan death grip and drags her into the frame after him. They exit. A pause, then –*

ALEX: Come on! Back to the shopping centre!

> *ALEX exits. WARRIOR begins to follow, then hesitates and comes to a stop. CAT stops with him.*

Scene 8

CAT, WARRIOR

WARRIOR paces back and forth, thinking hard and staring off in the direction ALEX exited. CAT watches him disdainfully.

CAT: What's the matter? Out of puff?
Don't worry, he'll be safe enough.
In fact, he's better off alone
The Skarg don't want him on his own.

WARRIOR: (*To himself.*) I'd better let the boy go ahead. He's safer on his own. It's not him the Skarg want.

CAT: I just said that, you big prat!
    Don't you understand plain cat?
    We're in a mess – and you're to blame.
    You brought the Skarg out of the game.
    It's you those monsters want to slay
    But Alex could get in their way.

WARRIOR: This whole mess is my fault. The Skarg
    followed me to this level. They're here to kill me, but if
    Alex gets in their way, he could be hurt too.

*CAT reacts with exasperation to this second repetition but
WARRIOR does not notice. He is deep in thought.*

So, the question is what am I going to do about it?

CAT: I would've thought that's pretty clear
    The Skarg won't leave while you are here.
    It's only you they want to slaughter
    So, listen, don't you think you ought to
    Take them back into the game?
    Just tootle through the way you came.

WARRIOR: Will you stop that yowling? I'm trying to think!

CAT: Thinking? There's a novelty.
    Try to take it gradually.
    Don't go into overload.
    Your head might swell up and explode.

WARRIOR: I have to take the Skarg back into my land.
    That is the only way.

CAT: The penny drops! Well, off you trot.
    Strike while that old iron's hot.

CAT stares at WARRIOR expectantly

WARRIOR: What are you looking at? (*To himself again.*) I'd
    better go right away, before the Skarg cause any more
    trouble. But, wait. This is not such a simple matter.

CAT: It can't be hard, even for you.
  Collect your Skarg and pop back through.

WARRIOR: I promised Alex I would not go anywhere
  without telling him first. I cannot leave without saying
  goodbye, but I put him into danger when I am with him.

CAT: (*To herself.*) Well! It seems he has a heart.
  He cares for Alex. That's a start.

  (*To WARRIOR.*) The Skarg won't dare to show their face
  In a bright and crowded place.
  A shopping centre rendezvous
  Is where you should say toodledoo.

WARRIOR: I know! I can say goodbye to Alex in the
  shopping centre! The Skarg will not dare to attack us in
  such a crowded place.

CAT: At last he's worked out what to do!
  It took so long my paws are blue.

WARRIOR: Hurry up, creature! We don't have all night!

  WARRIOR exits. CAT gives him a furious look before following.

Scene 9

ALEX, CAT, WARRIOR, SKARG 1, SKARG 2

*ALEX enters, calling behind him to WARRIOR and CAT. At the
same time, the two SKARG appear (disguised in Santa hats and
beards) in the middle of a crowd of Santas (or, they carry two life-
sized 'glove' puppets each – the puppets now dressed in Santa hats
and beards).*

ALEX: Look! There's Santa Claus!

WARRIOR: (*Hurrying on behind ALEX with CAT.*) Santa's
  Claws? Is it a weapon?

ALEX: No…

WARRIOR: A defensive tr–

ALEX: No… Come on! They're about to start the parade countdown.

SFX of a crowd and a garbled voice over a loudspeaker. All the actors join in the countdown.

ALL: Ten, nine, eight, seven, six, five, four, three, two, one…

Christmas lights blaze out. SFX of muffled applause and cheers. The actors join in, then line up at the back of the space, with the Santa Claus puppets and the SKARG. They all sing a close harmony, unaccompanied version of 'We Wish You a Merry Christmas and a Happy New Year' or 'Jingle Bells' or similar. The song ends.

ALEX: (*Moving to the front of the space with CAT.*) I love Christmas!

WARRIOR: (*Following.*) Why?

ALEX: Because it's such fun!

WARRIOR: (*Scanning the square.*) Ah. Forfun.

Throughout the rest of the scene, as ALEX describes Christmas, WARRIOR and CAT are gradually drawn into the picture he is painting. Behind them, the SKARG disappear through the frame with the Santas, then emerge again on their own, peering out, one on either side of the frame, still in their Santa disguises, listening.

ALEX: At Christmastime, everyone's on holiday. And there are presents.

WARRIOR looks puzzled so ALEX tries another word.

Gifts.

WARRIOR nods.

One of the best bits of Christmas Day is waking up and wiggling your toes and hearing the wrapping paper crackle at the bottom of the bed. And there's good stuff on the TV.

WARRIOR: TV?

ALEX: Television.

WARRIOR: Ah! Television! I like the television.

ALEX: And carol singing.

WARRIOR: Singing! Yes!

ALEX: And sometimes, on very special Chrismases, when you wake up, there's a wonderful quiet. Like the whole world's been wrapped up in a big, soft scarf. And when you pull back the curtain and look outside, there it is.

WARRIOR: What? What is outside?

ALEX: Snow.

WARRIOR: Snow…

He pulls out the snowstorm, tips it, and watches the flakes swirl. The snow/memory music plays softly. The lights could change to suggest snow – possibly a glitter ball.

ALEX: Me and my Dad used to spend all day out in the snow. Building snowmen, making snow angels, having snowball fights…

CAT: Nasty, cold stuff everywhere.
Give me a fire and an easy chair.

ALEX: A white Christmas. That would really be something.

WARRIOR: Will it snow this Christmas?

ALEX: I don't know. It doesn't happen very often. That's why a White Christmas is special.

The WARRIOR sighs and puts away the snowstorm. The music and light effects end.

But all the other things, they happen every year. We always have a family get-together on Christmas Day for a massive meal.

WARRIOR: Ah. Family.

ALEX: Don't be sad, Warrior. You can come to our house for Christmas Dinner.

He nods down at CAT, purring against WARRIOR's leg.

I mean, it looks like you're practically one of the family already.

WARRIOR and CAT both look round, freeze as they realise what they are doing, then spring apart in horror.

WARRIOR/CAT: Yeuch!

ALEX: You can have some of Grandad's beer. He won't mind. He always lets me have a taste. And there are crackers.

WARRIOR: What is a cracker?

ALEX: Well, you pull it and it explodes.

WARRIOR: Ah. So it is a weapon.

ALEX: No. A cracker isn't a weapon.

WARRIOR: A defensive trick, then –

ALEX: No! There are little toys inside. And funny hats. Oh, and there are always cracker jokes! Some of them are real killers.

WARRIOR: Killers? So, a joke is a –

ALEX: No.

WARRIOR: Then is it a –

ALEX: No! It's not that either! A joke is meant to make you laugh. I'll tell you one. Ummm. OK. What do you call a three-legged donkey?

WARRIOR: I do not know, Alex. What do you call a three-legged donkey?

ALEX: Wonky.

ALEX collapses with laughter at his own joke. WARRIOR and CAT (and the SKARG) are straight-faced. ALEX runs out of steam.

OK. Try this one. What do you call a one-eyed, three-legged donkey?

Winky Wonky.

ALEX again collapses with laughter at his own joke. WARRIOR watches him until he comes to a stop. WARRIOR then begins to laugh loudly but without humour. His face remains straight. He gets louder and louder, then stops as suddenly as he started. He looks puzzled and deeply unimpressed.

WARRIOR: Hmmm…

ALEX: My Grandad likes cracker jokes, too.

Standing, he stares in the direction of the hospital.

We're nearly there, you know. The hospital's just at the end of that road. Can we go and get him now? Can we bring him home for Christmas?

ALEX points the way. Behind him, the SKARG nod at one another excitedly and, as ALEX and WARRIOR continue to talk, the SKARG begin tiptoeing in the direction of the hospital, one on each side of the space. They meet up again at the front of the space, ready to head off.

WARRIOR: No, Alex. We must not go near the hospital. That is the one thing we must not do. The Skarg will do anything to capture me. If they realise there is someone precious to you in the hospital, they will take him, just like they tried to take your cat. They will take Maigran D'ad and once they have him, they will have power over us, because you love him.

ALEX: But – you'll come to my house for Christmas, won't you?

CAT: Tell him now. It would be wrong
To let him think you're staying long.

WARRIOR: Alex. There is something I must tell you –

WARRIOR is interrupted by a loud shriek. SKARG 2's volume control is misbehaving again.

SKARG 2: Neeeeeeeeee!!!

ALEX, WARRIOR and CAT spin round. The SKARG stop and look at one another, comical in their Santa hats and beards.

BOTH SKARG: (*To each other, fingers to lips.*) Shhhhh!
(*Turning to ALEX, WARRIOR and CAT.*) Shhhh!

ALEX: Skarg! After them!

Scene 10

ALEX, WARRIOR, CAT, SKARG 1, SKARG 2

A stylised chase scene, using all the levels of the space, with appropriate music (e.g. Frosty the Snowman). ALEX, WARRIOR and CAT pursue the SKARG, but the SKARG eventually escape off-stage. ALEX, WARRIOR and CAT stumble to a halt and try to catch their breath.

CAT: I can't believe you made me rush!
I must look awful, where's my brush?

ALEX: We lost them.

WARRIOR says nothing, just looks grimly in the direction of the hospital.

They can't have gone far. I know this shopping centre like the back of my hand. We can start the search over there –

WARRIOR: No need to search. I know where they have gone.

ALEX: Where?

WARRIOR: They were listening, Alex. They heard us talking about the hospital.

ALEX: My Grandad! And my Mum! She's there too, visiting!

WARRIOR: Hurry. There is no time to lose.

ALEX and WARRIOR exit in the direction of the hospital, followed by a grumbling CAT.

CAT: 'No time to lose – let's run some more.'
      This hero lark is such a bore.

Scene 11

SKARG 1, SKARG 2

The two SKARG enter, out of breath, still in their Santa hats and beards. They pull off the disguises, dropping them to the floor.

SKARG 2: (*Pointing to the big frame.*) Look, Sure. Moving doors. That is the entrance to the hospital.

SKARG 1: Good. We will enter this hospital and take the boy's my Grandad.

SKARG 2: It is a big place, Sure. How will we find him?

SKARG 1: I have been tracking that boy for hours now. I would know the smell of his DNA anywhere. It may take some time, but I will find this my Grandad. Once we have the old man, the Warrior will give himself up to us.

SKARG 2: How can you be so sure, Sure?

SKARG 1: He has grown soft in this world. He – cares! Have you not seen it? He would do anything for the boy. It's disgusting.

He shudders, then moves on, developing his plans.

Once we have the Warrior, we shall kill him. If he dies here, the portal will stay open and then countless thousands of our kind will swarm through.

SKARG 1 descends into an increasingly manic Dalek voice.

This – Earth – will be the next world to be conquered by the Skarg! Once we get rid of these humans it will be a fine planet for us to colonise.

SKARG 1 regains control of himself. He is embarrassed by his outburst.

SKARG 2: Do you have plans for this world, Sure?

SKARG 1: Plans? Yes, I have big plans. Decking. Lots of decking – and a water feature, of course.

SKARG 2: Oh, of course.

SKARG 1: I shall have outdoor lighting in the barbecue area – and all the plants will have unpronounceable names!

SKARG 2: Perhaps we should spare the one named Titchmarsh?

SKARG 1: Good idea. And you, Bus Stop. Do you have plans?

SKARG 2: I'm gonna go to Hollywood. I'm gonna be a star!

SKARG 1: How nice. Soon this world will be in our power, Bus Stop.

SKARG 1 pulls a stethoscope and a frilly, old-fashioned nurse's hat from his pocket. Handing the stethoscope to SKARG 2, he places the frilly nurse's hat on his head, unaware of how ridiculous he looks. SKARG 2 has some problems with what to do with the stethoscope, finally wearing it in a totally inappropriate way and talking into the end.

SKARG 2: Hello? Hello?

SKARG 1: There! Now we will pass unnoticed in this hospital. Come. Let us begin our – (*Shouting into the end of the stethoscope.*) – invasion plans!

They turn to face the frame. We hear the automatic doors open with a hiss exactly like the sound of the lift doors in Star Trek. This triggers one last Sky Movies burst from SKARG 2.

SKARG 2: Space. The final frontier.

SKARG 1: Bus Stop! That's another charge you're on.

SKARG 2: (*As Spock.*) Fascinating, Captain. (*As herself.*) It's not me! It's not me!

SKARG 1: When we get back home, you're going to wish you'd never been hatched!

They step through the frame. The doors hiss shut behind them. This delights the SKARG. They jump back and forth through the frame a few times, making the doors hiss open and shut. SKARG 2 jumps through into the space one last time, leaving SKARG 1 in the frame. Star Trek music, or similar, swells. SKARG 2 looks up into the sky, full of emotion, and smacks her clenched hand to her chest in a salute. SKARG 1 reaches out and grabs her shoulder in a vulcan death grip.

SKARG 2: Beam me up, Scottie!

They exit behind the frame.

Scene 12

ALEX, CAT, WARRIOR, SKARG 1, SKARG 2

ALEX, CAT and WARRIOR arrive outside the hospital. CAT in particular is very out of breath.

WARRIOR: Your cat does not seem very fit.

CAT: Oh, that man! He makes me spit!
     We cats don't need to exercise.
     What's the point? We have nine lives.

ALEX: No sign of the Skarg. Perhaps we beat them here.

For answer, WARRIOR picks up the Santa hats and beards, holding them out for ALEX to see.

Oh, no…

He looks towards the hospital doors.

Come on, Warrior.

WARRIOR: Wait, Alex.

ALEX: But my grandad's in there. And my Mum!

WARRIOR: What level is he on?

ALEX: Level? Oh, I see what you mean. He's on the eighth floor.

WARRIOR: Then we have some time. The Skarg will have to work their way through all the levels until they sniff him out.

ALEX: Good! That means we'll be up there ready and waiting for them. Take my Grandad? I'd like to see them try!

ALEX does some fighting moves with accompanying noises, then he comes to an embarrassed halt as WARRIOR watches him impassively.

What…?

WARRIOR: That is not the right way to end this, Alex.

ALEX: What is the right way?

WARRIOR: You must wish me back into my world.

ALEX: No!

WARRIOR: If I go back, the Skarg will follow. They have no choice. They will be sucked through the portal after me.

ALEX: But, I don't want you to leave.

WARRIOR: Alex. Earlier, you told me what it is to be brave in your world. Remember? A brave man does the right thing, even if he's really frightened. Well, now, I have to be brave. I have to go back.

ALEX: Why do you have to be brave? Are you frightened to go back?

WARRIOR: (*Striking a pose and parodying his earlier self.*) The warrior feels no fear!

ALEX: Were you happy, then, in your world?

The WARRIOR shrugs.

WARRIOR: I was not unhappy. But that was before I came here and learned about singing and forfun – and friendship. What will be worse, I wonder? To remember these good things when I return to my own world, or to forget them?

73

ALEX: You don't want to go back, do you? Look, maybe we could work out a way for you to stay…

They look at one another. WARRIOR clearly wants to stay too but knows he cannot.

CAT: (*To ALEX.*) Now don't start that. He must go through.
Don't worry, I'll look after you.
Before the Warrior arrived
My place was always at your side.
If he stays here, so do the Skarg.
And they're no picnic in the park.

WARRIOR: (*Turning away from ALEX.*) That is a kind thought Alex. But, no. I must go back, if I am to take the Skarg with me. And you, Alex. You must wish me back.

ALEX: Ah, now see, I can't do that! My handset got broken.

WARRIOR: You do not need it. The power is in the wizard, not the wand.

ALEX: But I'm not a wizard. I'm not magic at all –

WARRIOR: Everyone has magic in them, when they choose to find it.

ALEX: Do you have a wise saying for everything?

WARRIOR: (*Striking a pose.*) He who eats the dragon's eggs must ride the storm wind.

ALEX: What does that mean?

WARRIOR: Haven't a clue.

They grin at one another, then the WARRIOR grows serious again.

You must do the right thing too, Alex.

ALEX: What do you mean?

WARRIOR: You must be brave for Maigran D'ad. Don't take him out of hospital for Christmas. Take Christmas to him instead. Go and visit him.

ALEX scowls. WARRIOR waits.

ALEX: All right! I'll visit him!

WARRIOR: That is good.

He turns to CAT.

Farewell, Furball.

WARRIOR punches CAT playfully on the shoulder.

Sorry about trying to eat you.

CAT punches him back, slightly harder but still playfully.

CAT: Funny! Well, now. Toodle-Doo.
   You must have such a lot to do.

WARRIOR again playfully punches CAT.

WARRIOR: I had my eye on that nice, thick fur of yours!

CAT punches WARRIOR harder.

CAT: Whatever. Don't forget to write.
   Now go on, out of my sight.

WARRIOR punches CAT playfully.

WARRIOR: Still, I won't need fur now. Not where I'm going.

CAT: Will you stop that, you great lump!
   You don't know how hard you thump!

CAT punches WARRIOR in the stomach as hard as she can. She doubles over, clutching her fist. The WARRIOR hardly notices.

WARRIOR cheerfully gets CAT in the crook of his arm, squashes her face flat against his chest and knuckles the top of her head with his other fist. When she finally breaks away, she lifts her tail at him and stalks off. WARRIOR turns to ALEX. Reaching into his belt pouch, he retrieves the snowstorm and holds it out.

ALEX: No. You keep that.

The WARRIOR shakes the snowstorm and for a few seconds, they both stand still and silent, watching the snow fall around the man and the boy in the little glass dome. Then the WARRIOR puts the snowstorm back into his pouch and nods to ALEX.

Will – will we ever see each other again?

WARRIOR: Alex, I cannot come back here. Where I go, the Skarg will follow, and you may not be so lucky next time. But I will never forget you.

ALEX: How do I know that? How will I know you'll still remember me, once you're gone?

WARRIOR: I will send you a sign, to show you I remember.

ALEX nods, too upset to say anything. They hug, then WARRIOR gently disengages and steps back.

I am ready.

ALEX: But, what do I do? (*He thinks for a moment.*) Everyone has to say goodbye sometime, right? OK. Here goes. Goodbye, Warrior.

Nothing happens.

WARRIOR: I think you have to mean it, Alex.

ALEX: Mean it. Right. (*He squares his shoulders.*) Goodbye, Warrior.

The lights start to flicker. Dry ice begins to rise in the frame. WARRIOR music start to play. The WARRIOR turns to face the frame.

Goodbye, Warrior.

The WARRIOR walks forward.

Goodbye, Warrior! Goodbye!

WARRIOR steps through into the frame and turns to look out. The two SKARG stumble on-stage as though pulled by invisible ropes. They shoot past CAT and ALEX and head towards the frame, resisting all the way.

SKARG 1: What about my patio?

SKARG 2: I coulda been a star!

They step into the frame beside WARRIOR and strike a pose. The SKARG exit, but WARRIOR stays a moment longer, shaking the snowstorm and watching the flakes swirl in the little glass dome. Then he too, turns and walks away. When the dry ice clears he is gone, and the frame is once again the hospital entrance.

ALEX looks around, waiting for a sign from the WARRIOR.

ALEX: Come on, Warrior. Send me a sign.

Nothing happens.

CAT: Give him time, he's just gone through.
　　There's such a lot for him to do.
　　Check the post and feed his plants
　　Change his leather underpants

ALEX: Warrior? Show me you remember.

Again, they look around. Nothing.

That's it, then. He's gone and he doesn't remember me. Fine. At least I know for sure. Come on Snowball.

ALEX turns with cat and they walk towards the hospital doors. They are about to step through the frame when ALEX pauses, turns.

Goodbye.

We are unsure whether he is talking to WARRIOR or his father, or both. He turns back and the first silvery notes of the snow music start to play. ALEX and CAT stop, turn. A smile spreads across ALEX's face as he moves back into the space, followed by CAT.

Snow! Look, Snowball! It's snowing!

He spreads his arms and lifts his face, suddenly filled to the brim with pure joy. He knows now that he is not alone. He is not forgotten. There is still a connection. He and CAT move to the side of the space as the other actors appear in their 'people' guises, wearing hats and scarves. One brings the parachute silk. They allow the white parachute silk to rise and fall a couple of times and ALEX and CAT walk beneath it. ALEX watches as it settles to the floor, with CAT pawing at it to help it along. ALEX and CAT step onto the 'snow'. ALEX spins slowly, arms raised. CAT does the same. The other actors join them for a time, then kneel, facing them. CAT crouches against ALEX's leg. He puts his hand on her head, smiling out into the audience as the snow music plays.

Lights down.

The End.